CENTRAL AFRICA

NICOLA BARBER

A⁺
Smart Apple Media

First published in 2004 by Franklin Watts
96 Leonard Street, London EC2A 4XD

Franklin Watts Australia
45-51 Huntley Street, Alexandria NSW 2015

This edition published under license from Franklin Watts. All rights reserved.

Copyright © 2005 Franklin Watts.

Designer: Steve Prosser, Editor: Simon Adams, Art Director: Jonathan Hair, Editor-in-Chief:
John C. Miles, Picture Research: Diana Morris, Map Artwork: Ian Thompson

Picture credits
AP/Topham: 26
Bettman/Corbis: 16
Adil Bradlow/Trace Images/Topham: front cover top, 36
British Library/HIP/Topham: 12
EPA/PA: 31
Louise Gubb/Image Works/Topham: 37
Hulton Deutsch/Corbis: 10b, 19
Image Works/Topham: back cover, 39
Szenes Jason/Sygma/Corbis: front cover below, 29b
Richard Lord/Image Works/Topham: 41
PA/Topham: 33
Picturepoint/Topham: 8, 14, 15, 17, 18, 20, 32
Popperfoto: 21
Reuters/Corbis: 27
Patrick Robert/Sygma/Corbis: 30
Tim Rooke/Rex Features: 40
Sipa/Rex Features: 22, 23, 25, 35
Allan Tannebaum/Image Works/Topham: 29t
Topham: 11t
UPP/Topham: 24, 34, 38

Published in the United States by Smart Apple Media
2140 Howard Drive West, North Mankato, Minnesota 56003

U.S. publication copyright © 2006 Smart Apple Media
International copyright reserved in all countries. No part of this book may be reproduced in
any form without written permission from the publisher.
Printed in the United States of America

Library of Congress Cataloging-in-Publication Data

Barber, Nicola.
Central Africa / by Nicola Barber.
p. cm. – (Flashpoints)
Includes index.
ISBN 1-58340-607-7
1. Africa, Central—Juvenile literature. I. Title. II. Flashpoints (Smart Apple Media)

DT351.B2385 2005
967—dc22   2004065397

9 8 7 6 5 4 3 2 1

CONTENTS

INTRODUCTION

Central Africa is a vast region that extends south from the fringes of the Sahara Desert. It is bordered to the west by the Atlantic Ocean and to the east by the Indian Ocean.

THE RIVER CONGO

Geographically, Central Africa is extremely varied. In the west, the Congo River (once the Zaire) rises in southern Congo and flows in a wide arc north and west before reaching the sea. At 2,900 miles (4,670 km), it is the second longest river in Africa after the Nile. The Congo drains a large area of tropical rain forest. This area has a hot, wet climate year-round. South of the Congo basin lies an area of savannah. This rolling landscape has a tropical climate with wet and dry seasons.

THE GREAT RIFT VALLEY

East of the Congo basin runs the Great Rift Valley, formed by movements in Earth's crust that have caused deep, parallel cracks in the land. The Great Rift Valley starts in Syria and extends 4,475 miles (7,200 km) south through Africa to Mozambique. The

BANTU

The peoples of Central Africa speak many different languages, which are all related to each other. Bantu, the name given to this family of more than 500 languages, is thought to have evolved from a language originally spoken in the region of present-day Cameroon. Some of the main Bantu languages spoken in Central Africa include Swahili, Kongo, Rwanda, and Makua.

valley is between 20 and 60 miles (30-100 km) wide, with sides rising up to 6,500 feet (2,000 m) in places. South of Kenya, the valley splits in two: the western branch forms the eastern border of the Congo, while the eastern branch runs through Kenya and Tanzania. The two branches join again at Lake Nyasa.

East of the Great Rift Valley lies the Eastern Highlands. This grassland region provides grazing for domesticated herds and wild animals. A lowland area of coastal swamp, farmland, and long, sandy beaches lies along the East African coast.

FLASHPOINTS

Politically, most countries in this region obtained their independence from European rule during the 1960s. Since then, some have been largely peaceful, while others have acquired a reputation for violence, terror, and misrule.

The Great Rift Valley in East Africa.

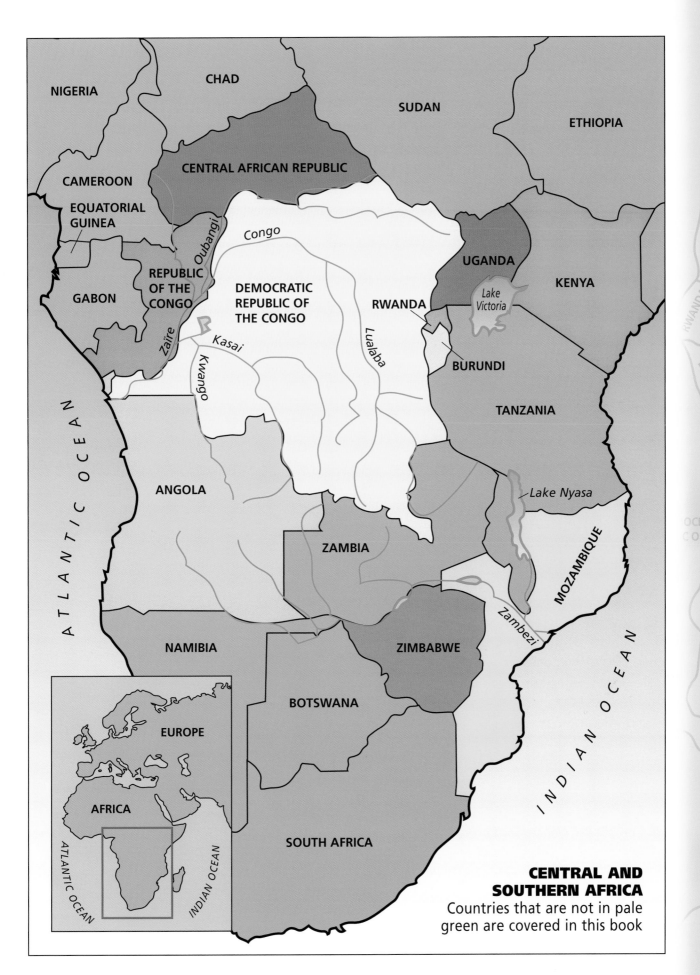

NIGERIA

CHAD

SUDAN

ETHIOPIA

CAMEROON

CENTRAL AFRICAN REPUBLIC

EQUATORIAL
GUINEA

Oubangi

Congo

UGANDA

KENYA

REPUBLIC
OF THE
CONGO

DEMOCRATIC
REPUBLIC OF
THE CONGO

RWANDA

*Lake
Victoria*

GABON

Zaïre

Kasai

Lualaba

BURUNDI

Kwango

TANZANIA

ATLANTIC OCEAN

ANGOLA

Lake Nyasa

ZAMBIA

MOZAMBIQUE

NAMIBIA

ZIMBABWE

Zambezi

INDIAN OCEAN

BOTSWANA

EUROPE

AFRICA

ATLANTIC OCEAN

INDIAN OCEAN

SOUTH AFRICA

CENTRAL AND
SOUTHERN AFRICA
Countries that are not in pale
green are covered in this book

EARLY HISTORY

Africa has been called the "cradle of humankind" because it is here that evidence has been found of the earliest human cultures. The first Stone Age Africans made simple tools for cutting and chopping. They later developed axes, scrapers, and arrows.

AGRICULTURE

Early humans lived by hunting wild animals and gathering plants that grew naturally around them. In some places, the most plentiful food was found in the local rivers and lakes. Here, fishing communities developed. Members of these communities made harpoon heads and fishhooks from bone and cooked fish and other foods in simple earthen pots.

The early development of agriculture in Central Africa was probably driven by a change in climate. Between about 8000 and 4000 B.C., the climate in the Sahara region was much wetter than it is today, and fishing communities were established along the southern fringes of this region. As the climate became drier and the rivers and lakes began to disappear, people living on these southern fringes began to domesticate wild grains by collecting their seeds and then planting and harvesting them regularly. The most important crops were sorghum and millet. In the forest regions of Central Africa, the yam was also domesticated. Farming led to the development of small, settled communities. As the food supply became more regular, the population began to increase.

People also learned to domesticate wild animals such as cattle, sheep, and goats, and to live off the milk from these animals. Raising cattle became an important way of life in the central Sahara, but as the climate became drier, the cattle herders gradually moved south. The spread of pastoralism, as animal herding is called, was affected by a bloodsucking insect called the tsetse fly. A parasite in the saliva of the fly causes sleeping sickness, a disease that can be fatal to both cattle and humans. Tsetse flies are found in wooded and low-lying regions, so pastoralism flourished away from these areas in the drier savannah lands.

BANTU SPEAKERS

Beginning in about 1000 B.C., Bantu speakers began to spread south, a movement that was to continue for many centuries until most of sub-Saharan Africa was populated by Bantu speakers. They took with them a knowledge of iron working, allowing them to produce metal objects,

The modern Khoikhoi people of south Central Africa are descendants of the first Bantu speakers.

GREAT ZIMBABWE

Modern-day Zimbabwe (see pages 38–39) takes its name from the kingdom of Great Zimbabwe, which flourished from about 1200 to 1450. The Shona people of Great Zimbabwe were farmers who kept cattle and grew crops. *Zimbabwe* is a Shona word meaning "building in stone": the Shona stonemasons used their great skill to build stone walls, creating cattle pens, terraced hillsides for crops, and elaborate enclosures for important buildings. Great Zimbabwe was very wealthy because it controlled the trade between the rich goldfields to its west and the port of Sofala to its east. Great Zimbabwe was abandoned in the 15th century, but the new kingdom of Mutapa soon replaced it.

The ruined walls of Great Zimbabwe demonstrate the skill of Shona stonemasons.

tools, and jewelry. As the Iron Age began, a new food, the banana, was introduced into East Africa, probably from Southeast Asia, and soon became a staple crop for farmers.

EARLY KINGDOMS

By the later Iron Age (after A.D. 1000), Central Africa was a region of small communities, many with their own specialities such as food production, fishing, copper mining, or salt manufacturing. Along the east coast, the Islamic religion had arrived with Muslim Arab merchants during the eighth century A.D. City-states such as Kilwa, Mogadishu, and Sofala grew up along the coast because of the wealth obtained from trade in gold and ivory, which were brought from the African interior and taken by Arab and Indian traders to Egypt, Arabia, and India.

As trade developed and the population grew, chiefs and kings extended their power. Early kingdoms included that of the Luba around Lake Kisale and the Luanda kingdom to its west. In western Central Africa, the kingdom of Kongo grew in importance beginning around 1400 because of trade in raffia textiles.

EARLY HISTORY

c. 2 million years ago (mya) Early Stone Age in Africa; simple stone tools made

c. 150,000 years ago Middle Stone Age in Africa; more refined tools made from stone and bone

c. 40,000 years ago Late Stone Age in Africa; development of tiny stone blades and a wider range of tools

c. 8000–4000 B.C. Last major wet period in the Sahara region

c. 7000 B.C. First pottery made in Africa

c. 1000 B.C. Spread of Bantu speaking peoples; start of Iron Age in Central Africa

C. A.D. 1000 Start of the later Iron Age in Central Africa

c. 1200–1450 Kingdom of Great Zimbabwe flourishes

c. 1300 Rise of the Luba kingdom

c. 1400 Rise of the kingdom of Kongo in Congo basin

c. 1420 Founding of the Mutapa kingdom

c. 1450 Founding of the Luanda kingdom

THE ARRIVAL OF THE EUROPEANS

In the 1480s, Portuguese sailors arrived off the coast of western Central Africa. They established relations with the kingdom of Kongo and claimed the uninhabited islands of São Tomé and Príncipe off the coast of modern-day Gabon.

THE SLAVE TRADE

The Portuguese established sugarcane plantations on both islands. The plantations, which were managed by Portuguese settlers, relied on a slave workforce. The slaves came from the African mainland, supplied by the kingdom of Kongo.

In the 1530s, ships laden with slaves from Central Africa began to sail from the port of São Tomé across the Atlantic Ocean to the New World. Here, the slaves worked on plantations, mainly in Brazil, which had been claimed by Portugal in 1500. The number of slaves taken across the Atlantic

A Portuguese fort on the Kongo coast, used as a collection post for captives shipped into slavery.

remained relatively small during the 16th century—probably a few thousand each year. However, during the 17th century, the Dutch, followed by the French and British, became involved in the trade, and numbers rose dramatically. New ports, such as Luanda and Benguela, joined in the trade.

THE EFFECTS OF SLAVERY

European settlers did not penetrate far inland from the coast, but the effects of the slave trade were felt deep in the interior. Slaves

BETWEEN THE LAKES

Several distinct kingdoms arose in the region between Lakes Victoria and Tanganyika. The kingdom of Buganda was based on agriculture, mainly bananas. Buganda dominated the region throughout the 18th and 19th centuries.

To the south of Buganda lay the highland kingdoms of Ruanda and Urundi (or Rundi), roughly modern-day Rwanda and Burundi. In this area lived two main ethnic groups: Tutsi pastoralists and Hutu farmers. The two peoples shared a common language and culture and lived in relative peace until colonial administrations began to favor one group over the other (see pages 28–31), causing resentment and hatred to grow.

were often prisoners of war, so power struggles between states fed the increasing demand for them. The Europeans wanted strong workers for their plantations; the resulting export of young men from Africa left many societies with an imbalance between their male and female populations.

To pay for slaves, Europeans imported guns and gunpowder, Brazilian rum, wool, and cotton cloth. The Europeans also brought new crops from the Americas, including maize, cassava, tobacco, beans, and peanuts. Cassava was particularly important and became a staple crop for the Luanda, Luba, and Kazembe kingdoms in the 18th century.

THE EAST COAST

Portuguese sailors reached the east coast of Africa in 1498. During the next century, the Portuguese attacked the various city-states in an attempt to gain a foothold along the coast. They established bases at Kilwa, Sofala, Mozambique, and Mombasa and tried to conquer Mutapa, which controlled the trade in gold (see page 11). Although unsuccessful, they did weaken Mutapa authority.

Beginning in the 1630s, Portuguese settlers established landholdings in the Zambezi valley. But in the late 17th century, Changamire, a wealthy cattle owner, used his trained army—the *Rozvi* ("destroyers")—to set up a kingdom on the Zimbabwe plateau. He restricted the Portuguese to their landholdings and prevented them from taking part in the gold trade.

> *"From our ships, the fine houses, terraces, and minarets, with the palms and trees in the orchards, made the city look so beautiful that our men were eager to land and overcome the pride of this barbarian."*
>
> Portuguese eyewitness account of the city of Kilwa before it was sacked in 1505

THE ARRIVAL OF THE EUROPEANS

1480s Portuguese sailors arrive off west coast of Central Africa

1490s Sugar plantations established on São Tomé and Príncipe

1492 Columbus sails to the New World, later named America

1498 Portuguese sailors reach the east coast of Africa

1503 Portuguese attack island of Zanzibar

1505 Portuguese attack Kilwa, Mombasa, and Barawa

1506 Christian convert seizes throne of Kongo as Afonso I

1532 First African captives transported across Atlantic and sold as slaves

1599 Completion of Portuguese Fort Jesus at Mombasa

c. 1608 Imported cassava and tobacco crops grown on West African coast

1620s Mutapa Empire weakens

1680s–90s Changamire suppresses Portuguese in East Africa

SLAVES AND MISSIONARIES

By the 19th century, the frontier of the slave trade had pushed far inland, often along river trading routes. The trade in slaves caused massive disruption as some people fought for access to the trade routes while others moved away in search of safety.

SLAVES FOR TRADE

By the end of the 18th century, Britain had become the biggest exporter of slaves from Africa. This changed in 1807, when Britain abolished the slave trade (slavery itself was abolished in 1834). Britain attempted to prevent other countries from exporting slaves by sending naval ships to patrol the West African coast. Nevertheless, the slave trade from Central Africa to Brazil and Cuba continued unabated during the early decades of the 19th century, only coming to an end after 1850. Within Africa, however, the trade did not die out. Slave labor in Central Africa increased, as slaves were put to work to produce food and new goods for export.

The commercial trade that replaced the export of slaves involved three main products: beeswax; ivory from African elephants, which was used for piano keys, billiard balls, knife handles, and ornaments; and, later in the century, rubber. Other products grown and processed for export included tobacco, sugar, coffee, and palm oil.

Different tribes became important in this trade. The Chokwe hunters of the remote highland regions of Angola used their skills to become specialized ivory hunters and beeswax collectors. When supplies of ivory ran out as the elephants were exterminated, the Chokwe turned their attention to rubber.

MISSIONARIES & EXPLORERS

Many factors led to the British abolition of the slave trade, including the fact that it was becoming less profitable. The campaign for abolition was closely linked to the growth of the evangelical Christian movement, whose main purpose was to spread Christianity. Large numbers of Christian missionaries went to Africa in the 19th century. Many attempted to establish "Christianity and commerce" in place of the slave trade. Explorers also played a role in opening up the continent. Men such as Richard Burton, John Speke, James Grant, David Livingstone, and Henry Stanley set out to explore the rivers that flowed from the African interior, still largely unknown to Europeans. Information from their travels was vital for the opening up of Africa to increased European commercial exploitation.

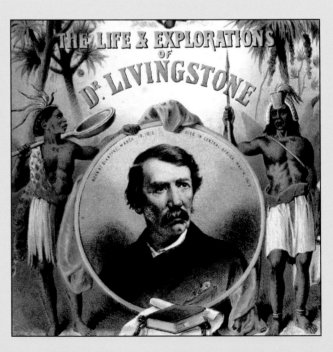

David Livingstone (1813–73), Scottish explorer.

THE EAST COAST

On the east coast of Africa, the slave trade was small-scale and local until the mid-1700s. Later, however, several factors led to a vast increase in the trade. French colonizers established sugar and coffee plantations on their Indian Ocean colonies of Mauritius and Réunion and imported slaves for these plantations from East Africa. With restrictions on the west coast slave trade, Brazilian traders also turned their attention to the east coast. This trade reached its peak in the 1860s before dying out.

The slave trade on the east coast went hand in hand with the trade in ivory, which also

The trade in elephant tusks for ivory went hand in hand with the slave trade in East Africa.

reached its peak in the late 19th century. The main markets for east coast ivory had been China and India, but during the 19th century, most ivory went to Europe. As the herds of elephants near the coast were killed off, the ivory trade moved farther inland. The main suppliers of ivory included the Yao and Ngoni people north of the Zambezi River, as well as the Nyamwezi, who lived even farther north. Raids for ivory and slaves devastated local farming communities and brought chaos to many previously prosperous and peaceful regions.

SLAVES AND MISSIONARIES

1788 African Association formed in London to promote exploration in Africa

1807 Britain abolishes slave trade

1808 United States abolishes slave trade

1814 Holland abolishes slave trade, followed by France in 1817

1834 Slavery abolished in British colonies

1848 Slavery abolished in French colonies

c. 1850 End of export of slaves from Central Africa to Brazil and Cuba

1860 Slavery abolished in Cuba

1860s Slave trade reaches its peak on east coast of Africa

1865 Slavery abolished in U.S.

1870s–80s Chokwe turn from ivory to rubber production

1873 Slave market in Zanzibar closes

1888 Slavery abolished in Brazil

SCRAMBLE FOR EMPIRES

Between 1880 and 1900, a great change occurred in African history as the European powers partitioned, or divided, the entire continent between them. Britain, France, Germany, Belgium, and Portugal all scrambled to lay claim to Central Africa.

THE BERLIN CONFERENCE

In 1884, the European powers held a conference in Berlin to try to reach an agreement over Africa. The conference was an entirely European affair; no African leaders were present.

The "scramble for Africa" was, in fact, well underway by the time of the conference. One of the events that had helped set it off was the interest of Belgium's King Leopold II in the activities of explorer Henry Stanley. On a journey that lasted from 1874 to 1877, Stanley crossed Africa from east to west, making his way down the Congo River to the coast and revealing to the wider world the vast, navigable waterway that led into the interior of Central Africa. Leopold sent Stanley back to the Congo in 1879 to oversee the construction of a road around the treacherous rapids on the river. In 1885, Leopold declared a large region south of the Congo River to be the Congo Free State, which became, in effect, his own personal kingdom.

In this fanciful painting, Henry Stanley is seen "cutting his way through the dark continent."

The serpent Leopold II of Belgium crushes the people of the Congo, as seen in a 19th-century cartoon.

SALVATION AND LIBERATION

The spread of European colonialism in Africa coincided with the development of independent African churches. The impact of colonialism had weakened the authority of local religions, and many young Africans turned to Christianity instead. Christian missions were often the only places that provided access to basic education and healthcare. Some African Christians rebelled against European domination and formed their own independent churches. One example was the Watchtower movement, introduced into Nyasaland (present-day Malawi) by Elliot Kamwana in 1908–09. It preached the second coming of Christ, a time when Africa would be liberated from colonial rule. Another Christian convert was John Chilembwe, who campaigned for equal rights for Africans and was killed after leading an uprising against colonial injustice.

RIVAL CLAIMS

Stanley was not alone in the Congo. In 1880, French explorer Savorgnan de Brazza made a treaty with Chief Makoko of the Bateke for land north of the Congo River. Using this and other treaties, France laid claim to Gabon, "Middle" Congo, and Ubangi-Chari (modern-day Central African Republic). Meanwhile, the Portuguese had ancient claims on Central Africa and could not afford to lose out in the scramble for colonies. Portugal was forced to give up any claim to the region around the Congo, but it established colonies in Angola on the west coast and Mozambique on the east.

Both Britain and Germany claimed lands in East Africa. Treaties between the two gave modern-day Kenya and Uganda to Britain and Tanganyika (modern-day Tanzania) to Germany. Both constructed railways into their new colonies but encountered fierce resistance to their rule. Guerrilla attacks against the British were carried out by the Nandi and the Mazrui in Kenya, while the Germans faced widespread resistance in the early 1900s from the Maji-Maji rebellion.

EMPIRE BUILDING

1874–77 Stanley crosses Africa from east to west

1879 Stanley returns to Africa as agent of Leopold II of Belgium

1880 De Brazza makes treaty with Bateke chief

1880s–90s European "Scramble for Africa"

1884–85 Berlin Conference divides up continent

1885 Leopold declares the Congo Free State

1890 Anglo-German treaty allocates territory in East Africa

1905–06 Maji-Maji uprising

1908–09 Watchtower movement introduced into Nyasaland by Elliot Kamwana

1915 John Chilembwe leads resistance to British rule

COLONIAL RULE

The European powers used Africa as a source of cheap raw materials to supply their industries. Many colonial governments leased vast tracts of land to private companies. It was up to these companies to exploit the natural resources of the region. Many did so through violence and forced labor.

VIOLENT OPPRESSION

One of the most brutal regimes in Central Africa was in the Congo Free State, where Belgian King Leopold II leased much of the land to private companies. The main raw material was natural rubber, obtained from tropical trees. Demand for rubber grew rapidly after 1890 because of the development of motorized vehicles and their need for tires. Workers for the companies used all means possible to obtain rubber at the lowest prices. Armed gangs traveled up the rivers of the Congo basin to attack villages, killing and mutilating the inhabitants and taking hostages until the required amount of rubber was collected. Many Africans deserted their villages and fled from the rivers to more remote—and often less fertile—land. African resistance and international condemnation of this system forced Leopold to hand over the Free State to the Belgian government in 1908, which brought some of the worst violence to an end.

The European owner of a rubber plantation watches as his crop is weighed in 1910.

WHITE SETTLEMENT

British-run Kenya was widely settled by white people. Here, as elsewhere, the interests of the white settlers were placed before those of the local African population. In the early 20th century, the British brought about 32,000 workers from India to construct a railroad from Mombasa, on the coast, to Lake Victoria. Thousands of these workers then settled in Kenya and Uganda and became involved in commerce. Largely to stifle competition from the Indians, white settlers demanded that large areas of fertile land in central Kenya be reserved for them alone. African farmers had also seized the opportunity to grow Arabica coffee, which was more profitable than the Robusta variety. Again, demands from white settlers led to a white-only monopoly on growing Arabica coffee.

Workers on a Kenyan coffee farm in 1953.

WORLD WAR I

World War I (1914-18) was essentially a European war fought between Germany and Austria-Hungary against Britain and its empire, France, and Russia. But the war also spread to Africa. France recruited thousands of African troops to fight in Europe, while Britain and Germany fought over Tanganyika in East Africa. It is estimated that a million Kenyans and Ugandans were forced to work as porters for the British army in East Africa, and at least 100,000 died in this service. At the end of the war, the former German colonies were reallocated by the European victors. In Central Africa, Britain gained Tanganyika, while Belgium obtained Rwanda and Burundi, and Britain and France divided Cameroon between them.

The postwar period saw the beginning of the exploitation of Africa's mineral wealth. In the Belgian Congo, rich copper reserves were discovered in Katanga. Since the region was sparsely populated, workers were recruited from many miles away. This pattern of migrant labor became a feature of colonial rule across Central Africa. Colonial governments imposed taxes on the African populations, forcing many African men to leave their homes to look for work in mines and on plantations, which were all owned by Europeans.

COLONIAL RULE				
1901 Most colonial boundaries have been established	**1908** Congo Free State taken over by Belgian government	Britain, France, and Belgium at the end of the war	places such as Kenya and Southern Rhodesia (Zimbabwe)	
1901–14 Colonial administrations established throughout region	**1914–18** World War I: Britain and Germany fight over German Tanganyika; Germany loses its African colonies to	**1920s** Exploitation of copper reserves in Katanga, southern Congo, begins; white settlers take land from Africans in	**1920s–30s** Early growth of African nationalist movements in the region	

THE ROAD TO INDEPENDENCE

During World War II (1939–45), Africa was once again drawn into a European war. The African colonies were a vital source of men and materials for Britain and France.

African colonial troops in the British Army help to build a bridge in Libya, 1943.

IMPACT OF THE WAR

The war marked a turning point in Africa; the rise of nationalism meant that African attitudes toward the colonial powers would never be the same again. Both Britain and France began to plan limited reforms, small and cautious steps toward eventual independence. However, it soon became clear that the colonial powers could no longer dictate the pace of change in Africa.

TANGANYIKA

One example of the power of nationalism was Tanganyika. In 1929, a discussion group called the Tanganyika African Association (TAA) established branches throughout the country. The use of the Swahili language made it possible for the many different ethnic groups to communicate freely and was an important factor in the move toward independence. In 1951, the TAA led resistance to an attempted eviction of thousands of farmers to make way for white settlers. In 1954, Julius Nyerere reformed the TAA into a political party called the Tanganyika African National Union (TANU). Progress to independence was swift. In 1961, Tanganyika became independent, with Nyerere as the country's first prime minister. In 1964, Tanganyika and the island state of Zanzibar merged to form Tanzania.

DECOLONIZATION

The various colonial powers had very different policies toward their African colonies. France tried to keep its colonies as part of a "Greater France." Many Africans were prepared to accept this as long as they were treated equally with French citizens. However, it soon became clear that this was not going to be the case.

In 1958, French President General Charles de Gaulle issued an ultimatum to the French African colonies. In a referendum, people could vote either yes or no to self-government under French rule. If the majority voted no, the colony would have

DATES OF INDEPENDENCE

1960	Cameroon (France)
	Central African Republic (France)
	Democratic Republic of the Congo (Belgium)
	Gabon (France)
	Republic of the Congo (France)
1961	Tanganyika (Tanzania) (Britain)
1962	Burundi (Belgium)
	Rwanda (Belgium)
	Uganda (Britain)
1963	Kenya (Britain)
1964	Malawi (Britain)
	Zambia (Britain)
1968	Equatorial Guinea (Spain)
1975	Angola (Portugal)
	Mozambique (Portugal)
1980	Zimbabwe (Britain)

complete independence, but all French support would be withdrawn immediately. Given such a stark choice, all of the colonies except Guinea voted to maintain links with France. But continuing pressure from the remaining colonies resulted in the independence of all French colonies in 1960.

Portugal and Belgium, meanwhile, had no plans for reform in their colonies. Belgium took drastic steps to keep the people of the Congo isolated from the move to independence in other parts of Africa (see page 24). Portugal was a poor country and regarded its African colonies as vital to the economy. Its determination to keep its colonies led to open warfare before independence was eventually granted.

Julius Nyerere (1922–99), president of Tanzania.

THE ROAD TO INDEPENDENCE

1929 Tanganyika African Association (TAA) formed

1939–45 World War II

1944 French leader Charles de Gaulle promises "new deal" to people of French colonies

1945 Fifth Pan-African Congress held in Manchester, Britain

1950s Mau Mau struggle in Kenya

1953 Formation of Central African Federation

1954 Nyerere reforms TAA into Tanganyika African National Union (TANU)

1958 Referendum in French colonies

1960 French West and Equatorial African colonies become

independent

1961 Tanganyika becomes independent

1964 Tanganyika and Zanzibar form Republic of Tanzania

REPUBLIC OF THE CONGO

Despite many changes in government, the first three decades of its existence as an independent nation were relatively peaceful for the Republic of the Congo. However, civil war now reigns.

MARXISM AND CIVIL WAR

The country's first president, Fulbert Youlou, was forced to resign in 1963 because of his pro-European policies. In 1964, President Massamba-Débat declared the socialist National Revolutionary Movement the only legal party. His government took control of industry and encouraged ties with Cuba, China, and the Soviet Union. A military coup in 1968 led to the establishment in 1970 of the People's Republic of the Congo as a Marxist state.

In 1990, the government abandoned Marxism and legalized opposition parties. The country's first democratic elections were held in 1992, but the results were

> **FACT FILE: REPUBLIC OF THE CONGO**
>
> **Colonial history:** Part of French Equatorial Africa
> **Independence:** 1960
> **Area:** 132,050 square miles (342,000 sq km)
> **Capital:** Brazzaville
> **Official language:** French
> **Population:** 3.7 million (2003)
> **Ethnic makeup:** Kongo 48%, Sangha 20%, Mbochi 12%, Teke 17%, others 3%

disputed, and civil war erupted. A ceasefire was agreed to in 1995.

In 1997, former Marxist President Sassou-Nguesso seized power. The civil war that followed claimed thousands of lives. A second ceasefire was agreed to in 1999, and a new constitution giving the president increased powers was approved in a referendum in 2002. A few months later, Sassou-Nguesso won the presidential election after his main opponents were barred. These elections sparked fighting between government troops and a group of southern rebels who called themselves "Ninja" after the ancient Japanese warriors. Led by Frederic Bitsangou (known as Ntumi), the rebels were easily recognized by their purple clothes. The fighting caused widespread disruption; an estimated one-quarter of the Congo's people were forced to flee their homes. A peace deal was signed with the Ninjas in 2003, and a campaign was begun to get the rebels to lay down their arms and return to civilian life.

President Sassou-Nguesso of the Congo.

The political history of the landlocked and impoverished Central African Republic has been tumultuous ever since it obtained independence from France in 1960.

INDEPENDENCE AND TYRANNY

A nationalist movement emerged in the French colony of Ubangi-Chari during the 1940s, when Barthélémy Boganda founded the Social Evolution Movement of Black Africa (MESAN) to fight for independence.

Boganda died in a plane crash in 1959, but his nephew, David Dacko, became the first president of the Central African Republic when independence was granted in 1960. Dacko ruled as a dictator, outlawing all political parties except MESAN. In 1966, as the country descended into chaos, army commander Jean-Bedel Bokassa staged a coup and overthrew Dacko. Bokassa declared himself president for life and in 1977 crowned himself emperor of the renamed Central African Empire. Bokassa arrested and murdered opponents and squandered vast amounts of the country's money.

COUPS AND CIVIL WARS

Bokassa was removed from power in 1979 in a French-backed coup led by Dacko. But Dacko himself was overthrown in 1981 in an army coup led by André Kolingba. Under Kolingba, the country moved slowly toward democracy. Elections in 1993 resulted in victory for Ange-Félix Patassé, a civilian, but tension between Patassé's government and rebel army forces resulted in violence during the 1990s. In 1999, Patassé was reelected, but riots in opposition to his rule broke out in 2000.

In 2001, former President Kolingba attempted a coup. It failed, but Patassé accused General François Bozize, his former supporter, of backing the attempt. When troops tried to arrest Bozize, fighting broke out between his supporters and government troops. In October 2002, civil war broke out again. Bozize finally seized power in March 2003. He promised to hold democratic elections and to begin to tackle some of the country's financial problems.

Jean-Bedel Bokassa at his self-coronation in 1977. His murderous rule as emperor was short-lived.

FACT FILE: CENTRAL AFRICAN REPUBLIC

Colonial history: Part of French Equatorial Africa
Independence: 1960
Area: 240,530 square miles (622,980 sq km)
Capital: Bangui
Official language: French (Sango is the national language)
Population: 3.8 million (2003)
Ethnic makeup: Baya 33%, Banda 27%, Mandjia 21%, Sara 10%, others 9%

DEMOCRATIC REPUBLIC OF THE CONGO

After World War II, the Belgian government operated a repressive regime in an attempt to hold on to its only African colony. Africans were not permitted to attend secondary school or to study abroad, nor were they allowed to form political parties.

SPEEDY INDEPENDENCE

Under pressure, the Belgians began to permit political parties after 1955. They held local elections in 1957 in which Africans were allowed to vote. Many regional and ethnic political parties were formed, but only Patrice Lumumba's Congolese National Movement (MNC) represented the whole country.

In 1959, riots broke out in Leopoldsville (now Kinshasa). In response, in January 1960, Belgium suddenly offered full independence within six months. African political parties were completely unprepared, and the whole system was thrown into chaos as Belgian civil servants returned home. Patrice Lumumba became the Congo's first prime minister, but within weeks, the army had mutinied, and copper-rich Katanga had declared itself a separate state. Lumumba was murdered in 1961, and the United Nations (UN) intervened in Katanga in 1962. The civil war that raged from 1960 to 1964 is thought to have claimed more than one million lives.

Prime Minister Gaston Eyskens of Belgium signs away the colony to Patrice Lumumba (left).

MOBUTU'S RULE

Beginning in 1960, Joseph Mobutu, an army officer, became an increasingly powerful figure in the country. In 1965, he seized power and ruled as a dictator, renaming the country Zaire in 1971. Mobutu headed a corrupt regime, receiving support from Western countries who preferred his strong rule to any possible alternatives. Mobutu raided the treasury to increase his personal wealth. By the time of his downfall in 1997, the country was bankrupt.

CIVIL WAR

In 1994, fighting in Rwanda and Burundi (see pages 28–31) sent a huge influx of Hutu refugees into Zaire. The presence of these refugees in eastern Zaire caused clashes with local Tutsis, who, backed by Rwanda, expelled the Hutus from the camps in 1996 and 1997. Under the leadership of Laurent Kabila, the Tutsi rebels then overthrew Mobutu. Kabila became president and renamed the country the Democratic Republic of the Congo. However, Kabila changed little and was unable to control the Hutu gangs still at large.

Another Tutsi rebellion in 1998, backed by Kabila's former supporters, Rwanda and Uganda, plunged the country into chaos once again. Kabila received aid from Angola, Namibia, and Zimbabwe. After he was murdered in 2001, his son Joseph took

Joseph Mobutu, president from 1965 to 1997.

power. By this time, at least 2.5 million people had died in the fighting.

A PEACEFUL SOLUTION?

In October 2002, the government reached agreements with Rwanda and Uganda for the withdrawal of their troops. In 2003, President Kabila agreed to a new constitution that provided for a power-sharing government for two years, with full elections after that time. United Nations troops arrived to try to keep the fragile peace. Yet another attempted coup in March 2004 brought renewed violence to Kinshasa as supporters of former leader Mobutu attacked the city. Additional violence erupted between rival groups in eastern parts of the country.

FACT FILE: DEMOCRATIC REPUBLIC OF THE CONGO

Colonial history: Belgian colony
Independence: 1960, known as Zaire 1971–97
Area: 905,570 square miles (2,345,410 sq km)
Capital: Kinshasa
Official language: French
Population: 52.7 million (2003)
Ethnic makeup: Bantu/Hamitic 45%, others 55%

UGANDA

The political unity achieved in Tanganyika (see pages 20–21) was an inspiration to other central African colonies on the road to independence. However, such unity proved impossible in Uganda.

DIVIDE AND RULE

Under colonial rule, divisions between ancient rivals had been deepened by British treatment of certain groups. The British had given special status to the kingdom of Buganda and to its *kabaka* (king). Before independence, Buganda's King Kabaka Mutesa II was determined to retain this special position. The country was also divided by religion; northerners were Muslim while southerners were Christian.

In 1962, the leader of the northern-dominated Uganda People's Congress (UPC), Milton Obote, became the first prime minister of independent Uganda. The UPC had formed an alliance with the Buganda nationalist party, *Kabaka Yekke* ("the king alone"). Buganda was given special status within Uganda, with its own parliament, and Kabaka Mutesa was made president of Uganda. But in 1966, Obote declared a new constitution in which he took over the presidency. In an attempt to impose political unity, government troops led by Idi Amin attacked the Buganda royal palace and forced Kabaka Mutesa to flee. Buganda was divided into four parts and absorbed into Uganda.

PRESIDENT AMIN

In 1971, Obote was overthrown in a military coup led by Idi Amin. The following year, Amin ordered all 60,000 Asians in Uganda to leave the country. Under Amin's military dictatorship, thousands of people were murdered and corruption was rife in the government and the army. In 1978, after part of the army mutinied against him, Amin

IDI AMIN

The year of Idi Amin's birth is not certain: dates from 1923 to 1928 have been given. He was born in northern Uganda into the Kakwa tribe and received little formal education. He joined the British colonial army in the 1940s, quickly rising to the highest rank possible for a black African. He was also an accomplished swimmer and heavyweight boxer. After independence, Obote promoted Amin to commander in chief of the army. Amin recruited members of his own tribe into the army and seized power while Obote was abroad in 1971. He quickly set about removing any opposition to his rule, and his "killer squads" murdered thousands of Ugandans. He also expelled Uganda's Asian community. When he was finally overthrown in 1979, it was estimated that up to 500,000 people had perished under Amin's brutal regime. He went into exile, dying in Saudi Arabia in 2003.

attacked neighboring Tanzania. In response, Tanzania invaded Uganda in 1979 and overthrew Amin; a year later, Obote became president once again.

Ugandan troops celebrate as they prepare to leave the neighboring DR Congo in 2002.

No Party Rule

In 1986, National Resistance Army rebels took Kampala and installed Yoweri Museveni as president. To prevent further civil war, Museveni banned multiparty politics, introducing instead a "no party" democracy. He addressed problems of corruption in the army and began to rebuild the country's shattered economy. Museveni won Uganda's first presidential election in 1996; the "no party" system was supported in a referendum in 2000.

Under Museveni, conditions in Uganda have improved considerably, but his time in power has not been without problems. Ugandan troops were involved in fighting in the neighboring Democratic Republic of the Congo (see page 25) in the late 1990s, finally withdrawing in 2002. Within Uganda, the army has to deal with members of a rebel group called the Lord's Resistance Army, which operates in the north of the country. The rebel forces consist mainly of kidnapped teenagers, and they continue to spread terror across large areas of northern Uganda.

FACT FILE: UGANDA

Colonial history: British protectorate
Independence: 1962
Area: 91,135 square miles (236,040 sq km)
Capital: Kampala
Official language: English
Population: 25.8 million (2003)
Ethnic makeup: Baganda 17%, Ankole 8%,
  Basoga 8%, Iteso 8%, Bakiga 7%,
  Langi 6%, Rwanda 6%, Bagisu 5%,
  Acholi 4%, Lugbara 4%, Batoro 3%,
  Bunyoro 3%, other Africans 20%,
  non-Africans 1%

RWANDA

During the colonial period, the Belgians used the Tutsi minority in Rwanda to enforce their rule. They deepened divisions between the Hutu and Tutsi communities by requiring all Rwandans to carry identification cards that stated their ethnic group and by discriminating in favor of Tutsis in government and education.

FACT FILE: RWANDA

Colonial history: German colony, governed by Belgium under UN mandate 1923–62
Independence: 1962
Area: 10,170 square miles (26,340 sq km)
Capital: Kigali
Official languages: Kinyarwanda, French, English
Population: 8.4 million (2003)
Ethnic makeup: Hutu 90%, Tutsi 9%, others 1%

ETHNIC DIVISIONS

The discrimination in favor of Tutsis changed in the 1950s, when well-educated Tutsis began to question colonial authority. The Belgians did an about-face and instead favored the Hutus. In 1959, Hutu riots, encouraged by the Belgians, overthrew the ruling Tutsi king. Many Tutsis were killed and thousands more fled to Uganda.

In 1962, Rwanda became independent, and a Hutu, Gregoire Kayibanda, was elected president. Tutsis were excluded from political power and were quickly blamed for anything that went wrong. Many more went into exile. In 1973, Kayibanda was ousted in a military coup led by Juvenal Habyarimana, who immediately abolished all political parties. In elections five years later, Habyarimana was confirmed as president. Pressure for reform led to the reintroduction of multiparty politics in 1991.

Meanwhile, Tutsi exiles in Uganda began to demand recognition as Rwandan citizens from President Habyarimana. They formed a rebel group called the Rwandan Patriotic Front (FPR) and in 1990 invaded Rwanda. The intention behind this invasion may have been to put pressure on the president, but its effect was to widen the gulf between Hutu and Tutsi even farther, and the country descended into civil war. This time, it was Hutus who were forced to flee as the FPR moved across the country.

GENOCIDE

In 1993, Habyarimana signed a power-sharing agreement with Tutsi leaders. But in the following year, hopes for a lasting peace were shattered by the death of Habyarimana when his plane was shot down at the Kigali airport by Hutu extremists (the Burundian president also died in the crash). This event sparked appalling ethnic violence, in which about 800,000 Tutsis and moderate Hutus were massacred by extremist Hutus. Many people consider this atrocity to be one of the worst acts of genocide in the 20th century.

In response, the FPR defeated the Hutu government, and the vicious civil war came to an end in July 1994. The FPR victory prompted yet another mass exodus of refugees; more than two million Hutus fled to neighboring Burundi, Tanzania, Uganda, and Zaire, where they lived in squalid refugee camps.

Tutsi refugees flee from Rwanda to Zaire along a road lined with bodies, July 1994.

DIVIDE AND RULE

The presence of so many Hutu refugees in camps in eastern Zaire destabilized that country (see page 25), and in 1996, many Hutu refugees were forcibly returned to Rwanda. Meanwhile, a UN war crimes tribunal began the difficult task of trying people who had been responsible for the atrocities of 1994. In an effort to balance the new government of Rwanda, the FPR gave some key government posts to Hutus.

> **"We cannot turn the clock back nor can we undo the harm caused, but we have the power to determine the future and to ensure that what happened never happens again."**
>
> **Paul Kagame, President of Rwanda, 2004**

Despite this, in 2000, President Pasteur Bizimungu resigned over attempts to increase Tutsi representation. He was succeeded by Paul Kagame. In 2003, Kagame won a landslide victory in the first general elections since the violence of 1994.

Paul Kagame became president of Rwanda in 2001. He won a huge election victory in 2003.

BURUNDI

When Burundi became independent in 1962, the Tutsi minority managed to hold on to power. The country became a constitutional monarchy under Tutsi King Mwambutsa IV. During the following year, thousands of Hutus fled as violence flared.

MILITARY RULE

Burundi's monarchy was overthrown in 1966 by an army coup, and Michel Micombero declared himself president. Unrest continued, however, and in 1972, large numbers of Hutus were massacred after an unsuccessful rebellion. Another military coup in 1976 replaced Micombero with Jean-Baptiste Bagaza, and five years later, Burundi became a one-party state. Bagaza was overthrown in 1987 by another Tutsi military leader, Pierre Buyoya. In 1988, tensions between Tutsis and Hutus again led to violence, in which 150,000 people died.

In 1992, hopes were raised as reforms were introduced by Buyoya. A referendum approved plans for a multiparty system, and a new constitution provided for a nonethnic government. The country's first presidential election was held in 1993. Melchior Ndadaye beat Buyoya to become Burundi's first Hutu president. Four months later, he was assassinated by members of the Tutsi-led army. The country plunged into civil war as another Hutu, Cyprien Ntaryamira, became president. In April 1994, Ntaryamira was killed with the Rwandan president in the Kigali plane crash (see page 28).

The arrival of approximately 63,000 refugees fleeing from the 1994 violence in Rwanda caused instability in Burundi. This photograph shows a Tutsi refugee camp near the northern town of Kirundo.

A BRITTLE PEACE

A third Hutu president, Sylvestre Ntibantunganya, took power in October 1994. But the situation in the country was out of control and was further exacerbated by the arrival of thousands of refugees from Rwanda. In 1996, Buyoya seized power once again in a coup. Talks to resolve the situation began in 1999 and continued in 2001 under the direction of former South African President Nelson Mandela. The outcome was a temporary government in which Tutsis and Hutus shared power. Despite these reforms, Hutu rebel groups continued to fight government troops.

In April 2003, Hutu Domitien Ndayizeye took over as the new president of Burundi, replacing Buyoya. Three months later, Hutus from the only rebel group not to have signed a peace agreement, the Forces for National Liberation (FNL), launched an attack on Bujumbura. About 30,000 people fled their homes. The rebels insisted that any negotiations to end the fighting be with the Tutsi-led army—which they said still held the

Former South African President Nelson Mandela (center) led peace talks in 2001 to attempt to resolve the Hutu/Tutsi conflict in Burundi.

real power in Burundi—rather than with the government. In April 2004, the FNL agreed to a ceasefire, provided that they were not attacked by government troops. The long-term objective is to absorb the Hutu fighters into the army. But this agreement is fragile and much work is needed before Hutus and Tutsis can work alongside each other in peace.

FACT FILE: BURUNDI

Colonial history: German colony, governed by Belgium under UN mandate 1923–62
Independence: 1962
Area: 10,745 square miles (27,830 sq km)
Capital: Bujumbura
Official languages: Kirundi, French
Population: 6.8 million (UN, 2003)
Ethnic makeup: Hutu 85%, Tutsi 14%, Twa 1%

KENYA

In general, the colonies in Central Africa that had large populations of white settlers endured a violent transition to independence. This was because the settlers were usually unwilling to give up control over the government and land.

LAND ISSUES

In Kenya, the 3,000 or so white settlers who farmed the fertile highlands (see page 19) dominated the colony and were determined to hold on to political and economic power. In the years after World War II, many squatter tenants were thrown off white farms in the highlands. In return for farming small areas of land, these squatters had provided an occasional workforce for white farmers. Increasingly, however, white farmers were using more intensive methods of agriculture and wanted to remove the squatters from their land. Many of these squatters were

Kikuyu. As a result of their grievances, violent action against white-owned land and property began in the 1940s.

THE MAU MAU UPRISING

Nationalist sentiment increased with the founding of the Kenyan African Union (KAU) in 1944. In 1947, Jomo Kenyatta became its leader and traveled the country urging freedom from colonial rule and settler domination. In 1952, Kikuyu guerrillas, called Mau Mau by the British, began a campaign of violence. In response, the colonial government declared a state of emergency and

Approximately 2,000 Mau Mau terrorist suspects await questioning by the police, October 24, 1952.

JOMO KENYATTA

Jomo Kenyatta was born near Nairobi sometime between 1890 and 1895 (the year of his birth is not certain). He was educated at a Scottish mission center and converted to Christianity in 1914. He took a great interest in Kikuyu issues; by 1925, he was one of the leaders of the Kikuyu Central Association (KCA). The KCA sent Kenyatta to Britain in 1929 to lobby for Kikuyu land rights. During the 1930s, he studied in London and, briefly, in Moscow. During World War II, Kenyatta remained in Britain; he took part in the fifth Pan-African Congress in Manchester in 1945. Returning to Kenya, Kenyatta became president of the Kenyan African Union in 1947. He was arrested in 1952 and imprisoned a year later for his alleged involvement in the Mau Mau movement. He was finally freed in 1961. As the first prime minister of Kenya, Kenyatta presided over a stable and peaceful country. He died in office in 1978.

arrested African nationalist leaders, including Kenyatta, who was jailed in 1953. The Mau Mau uprising was put down with great ferocity; thousands of Africans were killed. Although it did not succeed in achieving its main goals, the Mau Mau campaign demonstrated to the British government that the white settlers' demands were excessive and that black rule was inevitable.

INDEPENDENCE

In 1959, the state of emergency was lifted. Kenyatta was freed in 1961 and became president of the recently formed Kenya African National Union (KANU). In 1963, Kenyatta led his country to independence.

Kenyatta died in office in 1978 and was succeeded by Daniel Arap Moi. Moi declared a one-party state in 1982 and suppressed opposition to his rule. When opposition leaders formed the Forum for the Restoration of Democracy (FORD) in 1990, Moi outlawed it and arrested its members. Following fierce international criticism, many countries suspended aid payments to Kenya. By the end

of 1991, a multiparty system had been reinstated. In elections held the following year, Moi was reelected to power.

In an attempt to tackle corruption at the highest levels of government, Moi appointed anthropologist and opposition politician Richard Leakey to head an anticorruption drive. In 2002, nearly 40 years of KANU dominance ended when Mwai Kibaki of the National Rainbow Coalition won a victory over his KANU rival, Uhuru Kenyatta (son of Jomo). Kibaki pledged to tackle corruption in Kenyan politics.

FACT FILE: KENYA

Colonial history: British colony
Independence: 1963
Area: 224,960 square miles (582,650 sq km)
Capital: Nairobi
Official languages: Kiswahili, English
Population: 32 million (2003)
Ethnic makeup: Kikuyu 22%, Luhya 14%, Luo 13%, Kalenjin 12%, Kamba 11%, other Africans 27%, non-Africans 1%

MOZAMBIQUE

After World War II, Portugal was determined to hold on to its African colonies and treated them as overseas provinces. Emigration from Portugal was encouraged and thousands of white settlers moved to Mozambique during the 1950s. At the same time, an independence movement was gathering pace among Africans.

FACT FILE: MOZAMBIQUE

Colonial history: Portuguese colony
Independence: 1975
Area: 309,500 square miles (801,590 sq km)
Capital: Maputo
Official language: Portuguese
Population: 18.8 million (2003)
Ethnic makeup: Makua Longwe 47%, Tsonga 23%, Malawi 12%, Shona 11%, Yao 4%, others 3%

FIGHT FOR INDEPENDENCE

In 1962, activists from several anticolonial groups came together to form the Mozambique Liberation Front, known as Frelimo. Two years later, Frelimo started a war of independence against colonial rule.

Ten years of warfare led to independence in 1975, with Frelimo leader Samora Machel as president. Machel established a single-party system and in 1977 declared Frelimo a Marxist party. In the years that followed independence, Mozambique was drawn into the internal politics of neighboring Southern Rhodesia and South Africa. Because Mozambique supported the struggle against white rule in Rhodesia, a group of Rhodesians developed a rebel movement within Mozambique—the Mozambique Resistance Movement (Renamo)—to try to destabilize the Frelimo government. When Rhodesia became independent as Zimbabwe in 1980, South Africa took over the backing of Renamo in

retaliation for Mozambique's support for the African National Congress (ANC). In 1982, Renamo launched attacks on schools, clinics, and transportation lines across Mozambique, and the country descended into chaos and civil war.

The civil war continued throughout the 1980s, despite a short-lived ceasefire in 1984. In 1986, Machel was killed in a plane crash in South Africa; Joaquim Chissano

Samora Machel, president of Mozambique from 1975 until his death in a plane crash in 1986.

became president. He ended the Marxist regime in 1989 and in 1990 amended the constitution to allow for a democratic, multiparty political system. At the same time, the apartheid regime in South Africa was coming to an end, and its support for Renamo dried up. In 1992, President Chissano and Renamo leader Afonso Dhaklama signed a peace deal to end the civil war.

A NEW BEGINNING

In democratic elections held in 1994 and 1999, Frelimo returned to power under Chissano. Support for Renamo remained strong, however, and in 2000, riots broke out as Renamo supporters protested against the election results. Chissano decided to step down after his second term ended,

Floods devastated Mozambique in 2000 and 2001, submerging large parts of the country.

and Frelimo candidate Armando Guebuza won the country's December 2004 presidential election.

Mozambique is still recovering from the civil war that devastated the country. The situation was made worse when the country experienced terrible floods in 2000 and 2001. The drought that followed in 2002 brought many close to famine. Mozambique's economy may be booming, with many multinational companies investing in the country, but this wealth has not yet had an impact on the estimated 80 percent of the population that lives in poverty in towns and rural areas.

ANGOLA

Like Mozambique, Angola experienced an influx of Portuguese settlers during the 1950s. It was soon clear that independence from colonial rule would not be won without a fight.

A THREE-WAY FIGHT

Three independence movements emerged in Angola to fight Portuguese rule, and each received support from different sections of the population. The Popular Movement for the Liberation of Angola (MPLA), founded in 1956 by Agostinho Neto, drew its support from the mixed African-Portuguese population in Luanda and from the Kimbundu. The National Front for the Liberation of Angola (FNLA), set up in 1961, drew its support from the Bakongo in the north. Unita, set up by Jonas Savimbi in

Luanda, the capital of Angola, is situated on one of the finest natural harbors in Africa.

FACT FILE: ANGOLA

Colonial history: Portuguese colony
Independence: 1975
Area: 481,350 square miles (1,246,700 sq km)
Capital: Luanda
Official language: Portuguese
Population: 13.6 million (2003)
Ethnic makeup: Ovimbundu 37%,
    Kimbundu 25%, Bakongo 13%, others 25%

1966, was a rural movement supported by the Ovimbundu people. The three guerrilla movements fought a lengthy war until Angola finally became independent in 1975.

CIVIL WAR

With independence, a power struggle broke out between the MPLA on one side and the FNLA and Unita on the other. The situation was complicated by the interference of foreign powers. Cuba and the Soviet Union backed the MPLA, Zaire and the U.S. backed the FNLA, and South Africa backed Unita. With the help of Cuban troops, the MPLA expelled the FNLA and pushed Unita into the south.

The civil war continued throughout the 1980s. In 1987, South African troops invaded Angola in support of Unita. An agreement for their withdrawal, and for the withdrawal of Cuban troops, was signed by Savimbi and José Eduardo dos Santos (leader of the MPLA since Neto's death in 1979). But guerrilla fighting continued until 1991, when the United Nations stepped in to negotiate a peace deal. A new constitution abandoned the previous one-party system and opened the way for multiparty elections.

PEACE AT LAST

The first democratic elections held in Angola in 1992 resulted in victory for the MPLA. Savimbi rejected the outcome, and Unita resumed the guerrilla war. Another peace agreement signed in 1994 heralded the arrival of UN peacekeepers the following year. But an attempt to set up a power-sharing government in 1997 failed, and full-scale war broke out once again in 1998. The UN withdrew its troops in 1999.

In 2002, Savimbi was killed by government troops. His death opened up the prospect for peace. A few months later, Unita rebels agreed to a ceasefire. Many refugees began

JONAS SAVIMBI

Jonas Savimbi founded Unita in 1966 and remained a key and often controversial figure in Angola until his death in 2002. He was born in 1934 in the eastern Angolan province of Moxico, a rural region that provided the main support for Unita. Savimbi was seen by some as a freedom fighter and by others as a warmonger. Under his leadership, Unita received support from the apartheid regime in South Africa and from the U.S. In 1986, U.S. President Ronald Reagan spoke of Unita winning "a victory that electrifies the world and brings great sympathy and assistance from other nations to those struggling for freedom." However, when elections in 1992 resulted in victory for the MPLA, Savimbi refused to accept the result and took the country back to war, refusing to attend negotiations for a peace deal in 1994. Savimbi was killed in 2002.

to return home, but after 27 years of warfare, the country was in ruins and famine was a constant threat. In 2003, Unita completed its transformation from a rebel group into a political party when it elected Isaias Samakuva as its new leader. The next elections will be held in 2006.

ZIMBABWE

In 1953, Britain created the Central African Federation, made up of Southern Rhodesia (Zimbabwe), Northern Rhodesia (Zambia), and Nyasaland (Malawi). Pressure for independence grew as nationalist groups emerged during the 1960s.

WHITE MINORITY RULE

Two main nationalist groups emerged in Southern Rhodesia. The Zimbabwe African People's Union (ZAPU) was founded in 1962 by Joshua Nkomo with mainly Ndebele support. The Zimbabwe African National Union (ZANU) was a breakaway group founded a year later by Ndabaningi Sithole and Robert Mugabe with Shona support.

In 1963, the Central African Federation collapsed, and both Zambia and Malawi became independent. In Southern Rhodesia, however, both ZAPU and ZANU were banned, and their leaders were imprisoned by the British. Britain was determined to pursue a policy of majority black rule, but the white settlers wanted to retain power. In 1965, Ian Smith, leader of the new, white Rhodesia Front party, unilaterally declared independence from Britain. Although this act was illegal, the British took little action. Economic sanctions against Rhodesia were put in place, but South Africa ignored them and continued to trade with Rhodesia.

For African nationalists, it was clear that armed struggle was the only way forward. From 1966 until 1979, ZANU (and later ZAPU) fought a guerrilla war against white rule. ZANU was backed by Mozambique; in retaliation, Rhodesia destabilized the regime (see page 34) to cut off this support. This tactic failed, however, and by 1979, ZANU and ZAPU controlled much of the country outside the cities. The Smith government was forced to admit defeat.

ROBERT MUGABE

Robert Mugabe was born near Harare (then called Salisbury) in 1924. He was brought up a Roman Catholic, qualified as a teacher, and studied in South Africa and Tanzania. He returned to Southern Rhodesia as a Marxist and joined Joshua Nkomo as a member of ZAPU, leaving to form the rival ZANU in 1963. Mugabe became the first prime minister of independent Zimbabwe in 1980. Although Nkomo was initially part of Mugabe's government, he was dismissed in 1982, and many of his Ndebele supporters were murdered. Mugabe won elections in 1985, 1990, 1996, and, controversially, 2002. His land reforms attracted international criticism and forced Mugabe to withdraw Zimbabwe from the Commonwealth in 2003. In 2004, Mugabe announced that he would not run again for president when his present term of office expires in 2008.

INDEPENDENCE

Rhodesia became independent in 1980 and was renamed Zimbabwe. Robert Mugabe and ZANU won the first elections, and ZAPU leader Joshua Nkomo was also appointed to the government. However, tensions between the two parties led to fighting in the south. A deal was established in 1987 to merge the two parties to form ZANU-PF. In 1987, a new party, the Movement for Democratic Change (MDC), was formed under Morgan Tsvangirai to challenge Mugabe.

While many white settlers had left the country in 1980, the minority white population continued to have great influence, notably in agriculture. In 2000, roughly 4,000 white farmers owned 27 million acres (11 million ha) of the best farmland. In March, government supporters began to seize white-owned farms. Most people agreed that a redistribution of land was overdue, but the government's violent policy had a disastrous effect on agricultural output as work stopped on many farms. Drought in 2002 added to the problem.

Black Zimbabweans chant and sing as they seize a white-owned farm, April 6, 2000.

As the MDC gained support and Zimbabwe's economy collapsed, Mugabe's position became increasingly difficult. To stay in power, he terrorized opposition members and curbed freedom of the press. He was reelected in 2002, but the elections were criticized as unfair by both the MDC and international observers. The following year, Morgan Tsvangirai, the opposition leader, was arrested on charges of treason, which he denied.

FACT FILE: ZIMBABWE

Colonial history: British colony
Independence: 1980
Area: 150,800 square miles (390,580 sq km)
Capital: Harare
Official language: English
Population: 12.9 million (2003)
Ethnic makeup: Shona 71%, Ndebele 16%, other Africans 11%, non-Africans 2%

REGIONAL ISSUES

Many of the countries in Central Africa have endured years of warfare, including civil war. The legacy of the fighting can be found everywhere. War disrupts everyday life, forcing people to flee from their homes and their livelihoods to live as refugees.

During her lifetime, Diana, Princess of Wales, campaigned for a ban on the use of landmines.

EFFECTS OF WAR

War has a devastating effect on a country's economy: infrastructure is destroyed, and tourists stop visiting. In the aftermath of war, Angola and Mozambique have both faced the problem of landmines, which are small, lethal weapons that explode when someone steps on them or picks them up, causing death or loss of limbs. Mines are often forgotten once the fighting stops.

FOOD SUPPLY

Zimbabwe was once known as the "breadbasket of Africa" because of its rich agricultural land. Today, a mixture of disastrous political policies (see page 39) and drought have led to severe food shortages. An estimated one-third of Zimbabwe's people are now malnourished. Angola is now enjoying some stability, but it cannot feed its people. During the war, many fled rural areas, leaving land untended. Now, even those who remained in the countryside cannot farm because of landmines. In Mozambique, food shortages are largely due to crop failures caused by flooding and drought from 2000 to 2002.

AIDS

One of the biggest challenges for Africa is to bring the AIDS epidemic under control. AIDS—acquired immunodeficiency syndrome—is caused by HIV, a virus that attacks the body's immune system. HIV is spread from person to person through bodily fluids. There is no cure for AIDS, and the drugs used to slow down the virus are very expensive. In many countries, AIDS has been controlled by improved health education, but in Africa, millions have died. In countries where people are malnourished and where there is little healthcare, AIDS is rampant. But some countries, notably Uganda, have fought the disease. There, the number of adults suffering from AIDS has dropped from 14 percent in the early 1990s to 5 percent in 2003. This decrease has been achieved through a widespread education program.

THE FUTURE

"The state of Africa is a scar on the conscience of the world." These words, spoken by British Prime Minister Tony Blair in 2001, sum up the desperate situation in many Central African countries. In most cases, these nations are defined by artificial borders laid down more than 100 years ago by land-hungry white men in faraway Europe. In the Democratic Republic of the Congo, continued fighting sent waves of refugees into neighboring Burundi in 2004, causing problems for the fragile peace in that country. The political situation in Zimbabwe continues to worsen, while in Uganda, rebels in the north of the country have caused 1.5 million people to flee their homes. Despite hopeful signs for the future in some Central African countries, it is clear that within the entire region many flashpoints remain.

Uganda has succeeded in dramatically reducing HIV/AIDS infection rates by increasing health education.

GLOSSARY

African National Congress (ANC) Main black opposition organization in South Africa during apartheid. The ANC was banned in 1961 and began a campaign of resistance against white rule; the ban was lifted in 1990. Today, the ANC is the main political party in South Africa.

Amputee Someone who has had a limb (arm or leg) or limbs removed.

Apartheid Policy of racial discrimination developed in South Africa that gave power to the white minority and excluded the black majority; the system ended by 1994.

Bantu Name given to a family of more than 500 languages spoken throughout West and Central Africa.

Cassava Food plant grown in tropical regions. It has fleshy roots that are poisonous when raw but can be processed into a variety of products.

Commonwealth of Nations Association of countries once ruled by Britain.

Constitution Political principles on which a country is governed, often written down in a single document.

Constitutional monarchy Country with a king or queen at its head, in which the powers of the monarch are limited and defined by the constitution.

Coup Sudden seizure of power over the government of a country.

Democracy System of government in which the people of a country have a direct say in how their country is run, usually through elected representatives.

Dictator Absolute ruler not restricted by a country's constitution or laws.

Ethnic Relating to a group of people who share similar racial characteristics.

Evangelical Christians Christians for whom conversion to the Christian faith is an important part of their belief.

Genocide Deliberate killing of one nationality or ethnic group by another.

Guerrilla Member of an irregular armed force set up to fight regular forces such as the army or police.

Lobby To influence politicians and those in power by persuasion and argument.

Marxist Political and economic philosophy based on the writings of German thinker Karl Marx, who founded communism.

Migrant labor Practice of traveling away from home in order to find work.

Millet Small-grained crop grown in tropical and semitropical regions.

Multiparty politics Political system in which different political parties compete for power.

Mutiny Open rebellion against government or military authority.

Nationalism Loyalty to one's country; in colonial times, a belief in the right of a country to obtain independence.

Pastoralism Way of life characterized by the keeping of herds of animals.

Power Nation that has great influence over international affairs.

Power-sharing government Political system in which power is held by government and opposition representatives working together.

Raffia Fiber made from the leaves of the raffia palm, native to Africa.

Referendum Direct vote by the people of a country on a particular issue.

Regime System of government of a particular political party.

Savannah Grassland regions in the tropics and subtropics.

Socialism Political and economic theory in which land, factories, and other means of production are held under public, rather than private, ownership.

Sorghum Grain crop grown as a staple food in Africa and Asia.

United Nations (UN) International peacekeeping organization, founded in 1945 and based in New York.

War crimes tribunal Special international court that meets to examine accusations of crimes committed during wartime.

Yam Food plant grown in the tropics and subtropics that produces large tubers.

INDEX

A

African National Congress (ANC) 34, 42
AIDS 41
Amin, I. 26, 27
Angola 14, 17, 21, 25, 36-37, 40

B

Bantu 8, 10, 11, 42
Belgium 16, 17, 18, 19, 21, 24, 28, 31
Berlin Conference 16, 17
Britain 12, 14, 15, 16, 17, 19, 20, 21, 26, 32, 33, 38, 42
Burundi 13, 19, 21, 25, 28, 30
Buyoya, P. 30, 31

C

Cameroon 8, 19, 21
Central Africa
  agriculture 10-11, 19
  colonialism established 16-19
  early history 10-13
  European influence 8, 12-17
  geography 8-9
  languages of 8
  slave trade 12-15
  trade 11-15
Central African Republic 7, 21, 23
Chissano, J. 34, 35
Chokwe 14, 15
Congo Free State 16, 17, 18, 19, 21
Congo River 8, 11, 16, 17, 18

D

Democratic Republic of the Congo 24, 25, 27

E

East Africa 8, 11, 15, 17, 19
explorers 14

F

FNLA (National Front for the Liberation of Angola) 36, 37
France 12, 15, 16, 17, 19, 20, 21, 23

G

Germany 16, 17, 19, 28, 31

H

Habyarimana, J. 28
Hutu 13, 25, 28, 29, 30, 31

K

Kabila, L. 25
Kagame, P. 29
Kenya 8, 17, 19, 21, 32-33
Kenyatta, J. 32, 33
Kongo, kingdom of 11, 12, 13

L

Leopold II 16, 17, 18
Lumumba, P. 24

M

Machel, S. 34
Malawi 21, 38
Marxism 22, 34, 35, 38, 43
Mau Mau 21, 32, 33

missionaries 14, 36
Mobutu, J. 25
Moi, D. Arap 33
Mozambique 8, 13, 17, 21, 34-35, 40, 41
MPLA (Popular Movement for the Liberation of Angola) 36, 37
Mugabe, R. 38, 39
Museveni, Y. 27
Mutapa, kingdom of 11, 13

N

Nyerere, J. 20, 21

O

Obote, M. 26

P

Portugal 12, 13, 16, 17, 21, 34, 36

R

Renamo (Mozambique Resistance Movement) 34, 35
Republic of the Congo 21, 22
rubber 18
Rwanda 13, 19, 21, 25, 28-29, 30, 31

S

Sahara 8, 10, 11
Savimbi, J. 37
slaves, trade in 12-15
Soviet Union 22, 37
Stanley, H. 14, 16, 17

T

Tanganyika 17, 19, 20, 21, 26 see also Tanzania

Tanganyika African Association (TAA) 20, 21
Tanzania 8, 13, 17, 20, 21, 26, 27, 28, 38
Tutsi 13, 25, 28, 29, 30, 31

U

Uganda 17, 19, 21, 25, 26-27, 28, 41
Asians 19, 26
Unita 36, 37
United Nations (UN) 24, 25, 28, 29, 31, 37, 43
United States (U.S.) 15, 37

W

World War I 19
World War II 20, 21, 24, 32, 33, 34

Z

Zaire 25, 28, 29
Zambia 21, 38
Zanzibar 15, 20
Zimbabwe 11, 13, 19, 21, 25, 34, 38-39, 40